A Vision of Strength
The Michael Chronicles

By

Michael Irons

A Vision of Strength:
The Michael Chronicles

Prologue

If we discuss what it's like to have a family, I will say I have a good one. I was born into a household with my three sisters, mom, and dad. None of them were prepared for a child born entirely blind.

By the time I could get up and move around, my eldest sister had already left the house. My other two sisters had to manage my inability to see and struggled to take me out and do things as they usually did.

A Vision of Strength:
The Michael Chronicles

There were no expectations or rules for me. I had a smooth childhood despite my visual impairment. My education, however, came with some challenges.

My family supported me in nearly every aspect. The most unexpected support came from my stepdad. His presence and strength helped me through significant moments in my life.

From my perspective, life could have been unimaginable and filled with things I never saw coming. I managed to make the most of it despite my blindness. I achieved things people never believed I could. This is my story of how my disability became my greatest achievement.

Acknowledgment

I want to acknowledge my entire family, including my mom, biological dad, stepdad, and three sisters, *Lisa*, *Leanne*, and *Kris*.

I would consider my way of life a privilege. I have lived more than half of my life on better terms solely due to my family's strength and support. My sisters have faced the toughest times, but even during those moments, they made sure to look out for me as much as they could.

A Vision of Strength:
The Michael Chronicles

I can now inspire countless others to embrace life and seize every opportunity fully. This book aims to help everyone realize they can achieve more than they think possible. Societal standards and expectations should never limit anyone, and I have been living proof of this for over six decades.

Dedication

This book is dedicated to my biological dad, who inspired me to write and share my story. I would never have reached this point without his unwavering support and love.

A Vision of Strength:
The Michael Chronicles

Table of Contents

Chapter 1: A Fragile Beginning

Like many others, my life on the surface isn't much different. The only difference between me and most people is that I was born completely blind, meaning my eyes never worked. I've never seen anything in my life, but I've had many experiences that have shaped who I am today. This is the most I can say about myself now.

A Vision of Strength:
The Michael Chronicles

The better part of this life is having *someone*. One of the most important people in my life has been my stepdad. He came into my life when I was just 14 years old, and since then, he has been a big part of my journey.

At the age of 61, I'm doing better, especially living in my own place. The story begins by introducing my stepdad. I was introduced to my stepdad through my mom. She belonged to a religious group, and through her weekly meetings, she met my stepdad. He was there helping with the presentations. They instantly formed a good relationship, and he visited our home immediately after that. He would always treat us to a meal during his visits.

During that time, I was away at school trying to get my education. But whenever I came home on weekends, my stepdad would drop by our house and talk to me about what was happening at my school and other things we could discuss. This somewhat put me at ease. I never expected to form a bond like this with my stepdad.

Back then, my stepdad worked as a waiter at a restaurant in Oklahoma City. When I got home in December 1978, my mom decided he should move into our home. I almost looked forward to it because my stepdad spent time with me during the summer. Every so often, he would take me to his tiny house in a small town about 30 miles from Oklahoma City.

Then, we finally set a time for him to move in. My stepdad moved into our home in late July, which improved things for me. Once he moved in, he helped me with some things I might have had trouble with. I never expected him to look after me.

I eventually started school by the end of that summer, and he continued living in our home. We had another good summer after I got back from school. That summer, however, we faced harsh times. It was hot; *we could not sleep in our rooms.* I was unsure what to do at night when my room became too hot for sleep.

To my surprise, my stepdad put his tent in the backyard the next day, and we put a little fan in the tent. I laid out my sleeping bag in the tent and headed out to sleep there at night. In the morning, we would come into the house the next day, have breakfast, and do things together all over again.

That worked out well because I could go out and sleep in a cool place, allowing me to have a good night's sleep. That made my morning a bit better. But the house had no air conditioning, and the summers were extremely hot and uncomfortable.

At the end of the summer of 1979, my mom got our house air-conditioned, and things improved from that point forward. My stepdad continued to stay with us, and by then, I had graduated from high school, gone through college prep, and got into college. I got closer to my stepdad, and he continued to help me with different things.

School wasn't easy for me. I had trouble in school and started spending more summers at home, but those summers were a little more comfortable and not so hot.

It was still hot in my room upstairs. However, the lower part of the house was more comfortable and chill. Things changed that summer after getting through undergraduate college. My mum was diagnosed with breast cancer; *none of us expected this*.

My stepdad helped us with that with my mom as well. My mom died in 1993 after I'd finished college, having breast cancer that came back in her liver and her lungs. I may not have discussed it, but that phase was brutal. I was always there but could not see how she felt. This kind of pain catches up with you on a random day.

A Vision of Strength:
The Michael Chronicles

Towards the end of my mom's cancer, she took my stepdad aside and said, *"Would you help Michael when I'm gone? I don't think the help he got in school was very stable."*

This wasn't the only time she asked my stepdad to help me out and look after me; *she would ask him now and then.*

"I need you to be sure and be there to help Mike when I'm gone."

And he agreed to it *every time.*

He took me out to dinner the day after he agreed to it. After we finished our meal, he told me about what had happened. That was one *horrible* night. I had trouble sleeping that night. But at least my stepdad assured me that he would help me out, and he told me he would get a parental check for me, which I thought was a good thing at the time.

This was the actual time and the beginning of my relationship with my stepdad. My mom's health continued to deteriorate with her cancer.

My mom passed away the day after Thanksgiving in 1993. That's when my stepdad took over and helped me with things in my life. When my mom passed away, I had gotten out of college and was now doing a little bit of computer training at the *VOTEC*.

I ended up staying in school, which led to my stepdad continuing to work on his job when he had his psychologist with the *Yukon School Board*. He would arrive home one to two hours later than me.

Once he got home, we would figure out what we would have for our evening meal. Every day, we would talk a little about what we might try to do the next day, and that continued until I finished the computer training at the VOTEC. I ended up finishing it, and they tried it out. There wasn't any result, the kind we were expecting, and nothing came out of it. After discussing it with my stepdad, we determined that it would lead us nowhere and that we still had better options. That's how he was with me all my life.

I found out my stepdad had spoken about me with my mom before she passed away. He said he cared about me and wanted me to stay at his house. He also hoped I might move out at some point, but not soon. I felt relatively indifferent about staying where I was. It turns out that I still didn't mean what he said. But he told me he wouldn't try to throw me out or anything like that.

A Vision of Strength:
The Michael Chronicles

As I stayed on, it turned out that when I finished the school I was already involved in, I had no opportunities because the computer training, I received was for an operating system called DOS, which was already outdated. They were switching to Windows and had no screen-reading stuff for Windows.

But it turned out I was thinking I understood all that. He stood behind me and said everything was going to be fine. We talked more about some of that stuff and things like that. I wasn't fazed as it was one of those things that was just like the school I went through to get into college.

I got out of college, and there were no jobs because the programs that I had changed in graduate school had a reduction in force and a high increase at the same time, both occurring in Oklahoma. My stepdad worked with me when I got out of school and afterward, and he stuck with me from there. I lived with him for the longest time. I only moved out when he passed away. We lived together from November 1992 until 2019, *when he passed away, it was June 19, 2019.*

My stepdad was my support throughout the years—a quiet, steady presence in a life that always felt unpredictable. He gave me what I needed most: *someone who truly saw me,* even though I couldn't see the world around me. He never made me feel obligated. Instead, he showed me what it meant to be cared for without conditions and loved without restrictions. Now, living alone, I carry the weight of his absence and the memories of his time with me.

His patience, kindness, and faith in me are etched into every corner of my existence. It was through him that I felt that the world could be kind. Though he's now gone, he is with me in every action I take, a reminder that love, in its truest form, never really leaves you. It lingers nearby, quietly forming the life it touched forever.

Chapter 2: Ghost of My Childhood

My childhood is a blur to me. I was about three or four years old. I don't exactly recall my age, but that's probably when I first remembered things. I was living in a house on *Estates Drive*, and I was in *Norman*. I ended up being on the state side in Norman. The earliest memory I have is of my dad's mom and dad coming to visit.

A Vision of Strength:
The Michael Chronicles

They stayed there for a week. I remember talking to my grandmother and grandfather on my dad's side. They came to visit Oregon and stayed at our home. As I mentioned, they visited us for about a week and talked about different things. Then, my grandmother and grandfather left on my dad's side and went home. Their visit had a purpose, but I thought nothing of it back then.

Back then, my mom was trying to put my biological dad through school. It was not going so well for my mom, who also had to work at a doctor's office in Oklahoma City, and all this was beginning to wear her down. My mom and dad were having trouble because my dad had sexually molested my sisters, both. And he was what you would call a pedophile. And it was going on, and it had gotten bad.

My mom knew that she had to get both of my sisters away from my dad, one way or another. My next memory is being in our home in Oklahoma City and exploring the garage and different rooms.

The next thing I knew, we had moved in, and my dad was no longer around. I was living in our new home with my mom and my sisters.

A Vision of Strength:
The Michael Chronicles

It turned out that my oldest sister had left home. She was trying to attend college and pursue a few other things. Everyone was unaware of what was happening then, but I understood. It was me, my mum, and my other two sisters: my youngest sister and the one in the middle. Things were difficult. My mum had to work since my biological dad wasn't willing to pay for child support.

I started elementary school while living in our first home in Oklahoma City. It was a nice home. It had a 3-bedroom set. It turned out the house wasn't quite big enough for us, but we did the best we could with it. And I didn't know anything different because I wasn't old enough to understand what was happening.

I have memories of my sisters and me walking to work, with your mom and me there. Then, there was a swimming pool nearby, the office where we would swim. I also remember an unwanted trip to the doctor's office, as it was nearby. I don't recall what we did at the doctor's house, but I remember visiting my mom's office often. I was supposed to meet her at work and see the doctor about childhood illnesses that I had.

A Vision of Strength:
The Michael Chronicles

That was the first house in Oklahoma City, on 88th Street. Around 1974, when I was about 10 years old, my mom left her private job and went to work at a different one.

The doctor she'd been working for wouldn't let her buy the house, so we had to move out. In the spring of 1974, we moved to a new home in Oklahoma City. But it turned out that this newer house that we moved into wasn't new.

It was an old house that had been remodeled, but it was a new home to us. We moved there in the spring of 1974. It turned out this new house was larger. Instead of three bedrooms, it had four, and the rooms were even more spacious. There was a room for each of us in the house, which was good.

It was the first time I had an entire bedroom to myself, and my mom had her bedroom. My sisters also had their own bedrooms. I had some trouble running around the house in the beginning, but eventually, I learned my way around. It just took a while for me to do it.

That summer was not bad. It was interesting to get used to a new neighborhood and meet new people. However, at the end of the summer, I had to stay with my biological dad, which wasn't fun. I was very young when we moved away from my dad, so I don't have any good memories of him. I'm not fond of my dad. While living with him, I started school with the new school year.

It happened to be the *Oklahoma School for the Blind*, which was very difficult. I had a rough time there. This was the home that I would end up staying in from the spring of 1974 through the years that I was in school, in college, and then after my mom passed away. I'd only leave after my stepdad passed away, as no one would let me stay there anymore.

Chapter 3: Growing up in Altus

I was a fairly healthy baby, weighing about seven pounds. My birth went smoothly. Everything seemed normal at first. It was about six weeks when my mom noticed something unusual. She saw that the light reflected oddly in my eyes, which made her deeply concerned. Unsure of what was wrong with her son, she took me to an eye doctor at *Altus Air Force Base.*

A Vision of Strength:
The Michael Chronicles

After examining me, the doctor diagnosed me as blind. It was a devastating discovery for my family. My mom was overwhelmed with questions: *What had caused this? Could it have been prevented?* She pressed for answers, taking me to a hospital for further tests. Even after long checkups and tests, the doctors still couldn't pinpoint the exact cause of my blindness.

Eventually, it was concluded that some medication likely caused the condition my mom had taken during her pregnancy. This same medication seemed to have interrupted the signals necessary for my eyes to develop. My brain never received any signals, and my eyes never fully formed.

Today, when people look at me, they often notice that my eyes haven't developed properly. For some, this can be unsettling, but for me, it's just a part of who I am. It was never in my control.

My family's discovery that I was blind brought a new kind of fear. They weren't sure how to raise a child who couldn't see. Still, they rallied around me and focused on helping me thrive in any way they could.

I was determined to live as normally as I could. As a baby, I did all the typical things, from crawling and exploring to eventually walking. One of my favorite things as a kid was climbing onto the couch, holding onto the backrest, and jumping up and down repeatedly. This developed into a habit, almost a daily ritual, that amused me and strengthened my legs. Over time, due to all that jumping, I developed exceptionally strong legs.

While living in Altus, my mom decided she needed a change. She wanted a better-paying job to support our family, and my dad was bent on starting school all over, which led us to move places. We had to relocate when I was 3. We moved from Altus to Norman, Oklahoma. This move helped my mom to work for a doctor in Oklahoma City, earning better than before and allowing my dad to continue his education side by side

For many years, we adjusted to life in Norman. Adjusting to a new environment was another barrier for me. As a blind child, I had no other choice but to rely heavily on my other senses to understand the world around me. I learned to map out my spaces by touch and memory. I learned and gave new meanings to things around me just by touching them.

My family tried their best to create a safe and predictable environment, but there were still times when I stumbled literally and figuratively. I wondered why I was different from other kids, and though I didn't fully understand my blindness, I knew it set me apart from others in many ways.

During this time, my family faced many other bigger set of challenges. My parents' relationship became increasingly strained. My dad's education and my mom's long work hours put a lot of stress on their marriage. Eventually, my oldest sister moved out to start college, leaving the family dynamic even more fractured. My mom became weary of supporting my dad through school and began to feel that the situation was simply not in our favor as a family.

Things came to a head when my mom discovered troubling truths about my dad. We don't get to talk about it much, but as a child, I will never get to know the whole truth. I was too young to realize what was going on. He had been abusive toward my oldest and youngest sisters, creating nothing but fear and tension in our household. My understanding of the situation came much later, through conversations with my mom and, more vividly, through stories shared by my youngest sister once she was old enough to talk out loud about her experiences. None of them was ever that good.

A Vision of Strength:
The Michael Chronicles

The stress of these shocks weighed heavily on my mom. She carried the burden of protecting her children while setting aside her own feelings of betrayal and anger. By the year 1969, she decided to leave my dad and preserve our family's peace.

We moved all the way from Norman to Oklahoma City, seeking a fresh start and a life free from the turmoil my dad had caused. My parents divorced, and my mom took legal steps to secure child support for me.

This was not easy. It was a huge turning point for our entire family. In Oklahoma City, my mom worked hard to create a stable environment for us, while my dad's involvement was limited solely to occasional visits. Fortunately, these short visits were peaceful and helped me connect regularly with him.

Our move to Oklahoma City also marked the start of my early education. Initially, things were easier for me to understand. I was comfortable with my family and my house. New places made things a bit harder for me at first glance. Enrolling in school as a blind child presented its own set of challenges. Many teachers and administrators at the school had little experience working with blind students, and

A Vision of Strength:
The Michael Chronicles

I often felt like I had to prove myself capable, even within a space made for people like me.

Braille became my main way of reading and writing, and I dedicated myself to learning it. My mom wanted me to succeed, which meant she strongly supported my education, always ensuring I had the resources and encouragement I needed to thrive.

As I mentioned, it never got easier. There were many moments of frustration. I longed to do things independently, but there were limits to what I could achieve on my own. Basic tasks, like finding a new classroom or participating in group activities, often required constant assistance.

At times, I would feel a twinge of envy listening to other kids run freely, unaffected by the challenges I encountered every day. But these things didn't stop me from completing my education. I learned to adapt and find new ways to participate and contribute.

One of the most important lessons I learned during this time was to keep trying. My mom's strength in the face of hard times inspired me to no end. She showed me that setbacks didn't have to define my life. Instead, they could be steppingstones towards long-term growth.

A Vision of Strength:
The Michael Chronicles

My siblings, too, played a bigger role in my development. Though they were dealing with their own struggles, they often included me in their activities, helping me feel like I was part of the family's journey.

As I grew older, I began to reflect more on my blindness and what it meant for my future. While I couldn't change the fact that I was blind, I realized I had the power to shape how I approached life. I started looking at things in a different light. My family's experiences taught me the value of perseverance and not giving up. These qualities established a solid ground for confronting challenges associated with my blindness and other aspects of life.

As a family of four moving places, with little to no support and my mom as the sole breadwinner, I became grateful for many things early in my life.

Reflecting on those early years of my life, I realize how much my family's experiences influenced the person I've become. While my blindness is a defining aspect of my identity, it was never the sole focus of my life. I never let that affect my capabilities.

A Vision of Strength:
The Michael Chronicles

Those early struggles taught me to view the world not just through my eyes but through my heart and mind, and for that, I'm deeply grateful.

Chapter 4: Earliest Ripples

My move to Oklahoma City began with my sixth birthday celebration, and I started school at Lee Elementary School right away, a public school with many students.

I was placed in a special class designed for children with visual impairments. Some students in the class were completely blind, like me, while others were partially sighted.

A Vision of Strength:
The Michael Chronicles

My very first teacher, Mrs. Caldwell, had extensive experience working with blind and visually impaired students. She was kind and patient. I still remember all things about her, even though I still cannot comprehend how she looked. Despite her persistent efforts, I struggled to learn Braille.

I often got my letters mixed up and reversed. This difficulty also extended to math since numbers became confusing when reversed.

Mrs. Caldwell worked hard to help me understand Braille and improve my math skills. I made progress under her guidance, but it took me a lot of time. She was my teacher from first through third grade, and during that time, I slowly began to find my footing.

However, after my third year, Mrs. Caldwell retired. Her departure signaled the start of a challenging time in my education.

When I started fourth grade, the new teacher assigned to our class had little experience working with blind and partially sighted students. This lack of expertise made it tough to keep up with my lessons.

A Vision of Strength:
The Michael Chronicles

This was my initial downfall, and I fell behind in reading and math. By the time I entered fifth grade, the situation had worsened. My fifth-grade teacher spent most of her time in the teacher's lounge, leaving the older students in charge of the class.

Sometimes, I was put in charge, even though I had no idea what we were supposed to be working on. Because of that reason, our class accomplished very little. My battle with Braille and math continued to grow, and I fell even further behind.

When my mom and sisters learned about the lack of structure in my education, they were furious. They confronted the school, but the damage had already been done. At the end of the year, my fifth-grade teacher transferred to another school. Fortunately, my sixth-grade teacher was more knowledgeable and dedicated. She worked with me and my classmates on Braille, math, and other subjects.

After my sixth-grade year, my parents decided that I needed a more specialized learning environment. They enrolled me at the Oklahoma School for the Blind (OSB) in Muskogee, Oklahoma. That summer was relatively much better but as the start of the school year approached, I felt a mix of anxiety and hope. At twelve years old, transitioning to a new school was an uncomfortable experience, especially one where I would live away from my family.

At OSB, I found it difficult to adjust. I was placed in a group of students who had already been together for years. They had formed close bonds, and I felt like an outsider.

Some teased me, calling me slow and criticizing how I did things. They made me feel like I had been doing things wrong all my life.

Their constant ridicule made me feel isolated. The transition to a new environment and the teasing made my first year at OSB extremely difficult.

If we remove these things, OSB has excellent teachers committed to helping students accomplish almost everything. One of my teachers, *Mrs. Carter*, quickly identified the gaps in my education. She informed me that I was about two years behind in both reading and math. Instead of focusing on my shortcomings, she offered a long-term solution. Mrs. Carter told me that if I stayed after school, she would work with me to help me catch up. I took her up on her offer and spent countless afternoons practicing Braille and improving my reading skills.

Now, this was the part of my life where I actually looked forward to learning things.

Another teacher, *Mrs. Morris*, worked with me on math. She set aside time after lunch to help me understand math concepts and solve problems. Mrs. Carter and Mrs. Morris were patient and encouraging, and their dedication paid off. By the end of the year, I had made noticeable progress in both subjects. I wouldn't be that far in life if it weren't for them.

In my sixth-grade year at OSB, I continued to receive extra support. I started in remedial reading, attending sessions five days a week. As I improved, the sessions were reduced to four days a week to accommodate another student who needed help.

The balance worked well, and I gradually became more confident in my reading abilities. However, one challenge remained: *using a Braille writing tool called the slate and stylus*. This tool required writing letters backward, which I struggled with. No matter how much I practiced, I couldn't master it. Teachers and others assumed I wasn't trying hard enough, but the truth was that I simply couldn't process the letters that way.

Years later, my dad and I discussed my difficulties reversing letters in Braille. He suggested that I might have a form of dyslexia similar to what sighted individuals experience with reading and writing.

Unfortunately, we were never able to get formal testing or a definitive diagnosis. I caught up in Braille reading and writing with the help of dedicated teachers like *Mrs. Carter, Mrs. Morris, and later, Mrs. Weaver.*

While I eventually caught up in many areas, my struggles with Braille left a lasting impact. To this day, I'm a slow reader, especially when working with large amounts of Braille text. I can handle smaller sections but find extensive reading tasks overwhelming. But the support and guidance I received at OSB allowed me to keep up with my friends in other ways.

As I progressed through elementary, junior, and high school, I remained in regular programs alongside other blind and partially sighted students. My teachers' dedication and the skills I developed at OSB paved the way for my future success. They helped me overcome academic challenges and taught me resilience and determination.

The teachers who actively believed in me and took the time to help me catch up played a crucial role in shaping my life. Their positive behavior provided me with the tools and confidence to seek higher education and navigate the world as a legally blind person.

My experiences taught me the importance of persistence from day one and the value of supportive educators. While my blindness and difficulties with Braille presented unique tasks, they changed my life in many ways.

I've learned to adjust, stand up for myself, and appreciate the power of overcoming challenges. Although the journey was not simple, it equipped me with the challenges and possibilities that await.

Chapter 5: First Milestones

Certain moments in life keep you going through many things. For many, it's usually life itself, relationships, and family. While I had good family support growing up, my other moment was overcoming things deemed impossible for me by the masses.

I can only completely reflect on my thoughts and experiences by discussing them. I now recognize how major and minor events have shaped me into who I am today.

A Vision of Strength:
The Michael Chronicles

Some moments stand out more than others, not solely due to their grandness but their significance to me at the time.

My earliest achievements date back to elementary school. In 4th grade, we all took spelling tests and got lists of words to learn how to spell every week. I became pretty good at spelling, and I truly enjoyed learning at that moment. Then we had a spelling contest. The first one I got was Chelsea for being the best speller in my class, and that was in 4th grade. I was delighted to receive that.

With many more years to come, my next achievement was wrestling. Now, that is indeed quite different from standard academic accomplishments, but this one stands out as I poured all my effort into it. This was during my time in the junior high school band. I got a third-place medal in a wrestling match with the *Kansas School* for the *Blind*. I was wrestling with a guy from a Canadian school, and I lost that match.

I beat the very first guy I wrestled with. The next guy I wrestled beat me, but he had to work for it. The next guy also managed to beat me, but I made him work for it. We wrestled for close to three or four minutes. In the end, I didn't get to go to any of the places we were competing, but I felt good knowing that I had made them earn their wins.

The year continued in junior high school, and we had some wrestling contests among our team members. We had to wrestle with each other to see who would go to different competitions.

We had more wrestling practices, and then it came time to decide who would go to the big wrestling meet in Illinois. I wasn't able to go, but the coach took me aside after a meeting and told me that I worked really hard.

At the end of the year, I received the Coaches Award in recognition of my effort and determination. Even though I lost my matches, I made my opponents work for their victories, which felt pretty good.

When I entered my second year of junior high school, I chose not to wrestle because I wanted to improve my grades. I started spending more time studying. I was also involved in the junior high school band, which fit me better.

I started out by playing the baritone horn, but the very same teacher later switched me to a valve trombone, which I stuck with. I picked up a few song parts, but then the band teacher left at the end of junior high. For a couple of years, we didn't have a band.

Eventually, we got a new band teacher who began making efforts to bring things back together. At the time, I was in the chorus and informed him that I had played the trombone. He encouraged me to return to the band, and when I did, he asked me to try my hands out on a few different instruments.

I was then asked to play the tuba, which I thought sounded fun. I got back into the band and played the tuba. At the end of the school year, I got an award for my progress on the instrument.

Later, I joined the brass choir, where we played "*Never on Sunday*" and "*Great Is My Faithfulness.*" I enjoyed my time in the brass choir, even though we didn't get around to learning other songs.

By then, I had received two awards, one in my junior year and one in my senior year. I graduated from high school in 1983, and with that, my band career was over.

It's incredible to think about it. All the people who made fun of me for studying could have beaten me if they had put in the effort. I never held it against them. I loved them the same but felt a deep sense of accomplishment for earning that award. I graduated from high school in May of 1983.

After high school, I participated in a college prep program where I took an English course to prepare for college. Once in college, the awards were a little different. When I first started undergraduate school, I received the Scottish Rite scholarship.

This scholarship provided me with about $1,600 per semester, which helped tremendously. The *Scottish Rite* scholarship started towards the end of my freshman year. It continued for the rest of my time in undergraduate school, even into graduate school, until my very last semester.

One thing that changed for me in college was receiving another scholarship when I entered graduate school. This was a graduate stipend, and I was paid $162 a month for my last semester just for being in school. During my final year of graduate school, I secured the full graduate stipend, which paid me a little over $300 monthly. This was a huge help, especially when I had to leave East Central University to complete my internship in different locations.

When I did my internship in Dallas, Texas, I also received financial assistance from the state of Oklahoma. They provided me with $500 a month for four months in Dallas. That financial support made my internship possible and guaranteed that I could finish my graduate program.

These scholarships and stipends were major achievements for me, especially given that I have been blind since birth. They enabled me to pursue my education with fewer financial barriers and provided the support I needed to succeed. Each accomplishment symbolizes my hard work and determination throughout my academic journey.

Only by writing down my experiences did I realize that every award, every scholarship, and every late night spent studying was more than just an academic achievement; *it was proof of my resilience.*

While others could take certain things for granted, I had to find my own ways to make things work, and I did. Being named salutatorian, earning scholarships, and completing my internship were all milestones that reminded me of what was possible with determination. I still carry that pride with me today, knowing that no matter the challenges I pushed through, which made all the difference.

While not everything turned out exactly as I had planned, each experience helped me grow in unexpected ways.

A Vision of Strength:
The Michael Chronicles

Whether it was wrestling, music, academics, or career training, I kept moving forward, learning something from each opportunity. Even when things didn't go my way, I found a way out of it and made the best of what was in front of me. Looking back now, I feel good about the journey I've taken.

Chapter 6: Salutatorian Honors

From the very start, school was more than just academics for me; *it was a daily battle of trudging my way toward a world that was not built with someone like me in mind*. Being blind since birth meant that every achievement required extra effort, extra planning, and, often, extra patience. Knowing me, I was always *determined.*

I wanted to prove to myself, and maybe everyone else, that my blindness wouldn't hold back my success.

My next set of achievements started right away in college, which began in the spring of 1984. I earned a bachelor's degree in history with a minor in *Sociology*. When it was time to graduate, I was ready to leave school, but my parents and some staff members encouraged me to consider graduate school.

I was burned out from my bachelor's program, but I also knew that my job opportunities were limited if I quit. I didn't want to work at the *Lake for the Blind* or a vending stand, so I stayed and pursued a graduate degree in counseling.

The graduate program was a two-year program, and to be considered full-time, I had to take nine hours per semester. This was the troubling part, as I didn't have the option to make choices here. After two semesters, I was burned out and took a break for one semester. I looked into other opportunities but eventually decided to return and finish graduate school. I had two semesters left. The first semester wasn't too bad, and I almost enjoyed it.

After that semester, people suggested I try summer school. Then, when I talked to my graduate adviser, he said, *"You really should go to summer school because I'm going to be teaching a course this summer that you need to take."* That made that decision for me, and so, I enrolled.

A Vision of Strength:
The Michael Chronicles

Initially, I planned to take just one course, but my advisor suggested I take another class called, "*Characteristics of Mental Retardatio*n," which was done by appointment. I had to write a paper on the topic.

Summer school turned out to be enjoyable. The pace was slower, and I got to visit with other students. A close friend from the School for the Blind was also taking summer courses, and it was nice to spend time with him. Towards the end of summer, my professor suggested I visit *Palm Valley*, a school for the mentally retarded, to gather material for my paper.

I interviewed two staff members and completed my paper, staying at school till the first week of July to finish it. After the holiday, I went home and enjoyed the rest of the summer. My stepdad helped me format and print my paper, which I mailed to my advisor. I ended up getting a B, which I was satisfied with.

After summer school, I had one last semester of coursework, which was tough. I had to take two classes at the same time: *counseling with the personal, social, and psychological aspects of disability*. One of my classes was conducted "*by appointment*," where I met with the professor one-on-one instead of attending a regular class. That worked out fine. I listened to my tapes, asked questions, and managed my coursework. Then, it was time for my internship, which was required to complete my master's degree.

I was originally supposed to go to *Indiana,* Oklahoma, but the state office rejected my placement. Instead, I went to *McAlester,* Oklahoma. However, I couldn't complete my internship there due to a lack of resources.

I had no one to read materials for me and no way to visit clients. Once my advisor saw my situation, he decided to stop my internship. I got partial credit for my time there, but we needed to find another solution.

Eventually, I was sent to Texas to complete my internship at the *Texas Commission* for the Blind in Dallas. That turned out to be a great experience. The office was large, and my supervisor helped set things up for me. I had someone to read materials for me and even arranged transportation so I could visit clients. Everything worked out as needed, and I completed my internship.

Being blind, I always had to pick my battles wisely. I picked up things slower than the people around me.

A Vision of Strength:
The Michael Chronicles

Eventually, I made my way from school to college, and most of that was due to the great teachers who supported me throughout this journey.

After graduating, I completed computer operations training at *VIN Tech* in Oklahoma City. Unfortunately, the training became outdated quickly because the industry was shifting from DOS to Windows, which didn't have screen-reading software yet. Although I couldn't use what I had learned, I was still glad I had gone through the training.

I ended up getting some applications. It all worked out the way it needed to. I had a supervisor from the Texas Commission Office, and then I also had another guy who was in charge of my day-to-day Internet activities. They both worked with me. They finished my internship.

From learning new study methods to figuring out how to transport my tuba across campus to staying up late to ensure my grades stayed high, I faced every obstacle head-on.

When I started high school, I made the honor roll every semester. Most of the time, I was on what they called the B honor roll. I was surprised and tickled that I didn't make it every semester because I thought this couldn't be the case, but it was. From my first high school semester until graduation, I was consistently on the B honor roll. During my 9th and 10th grade years, I was also on the VR roll for about two years.

There were a couple of semesters, one during my junior year and another during my senior year, when I made the A honor roll. I was excited that I was able to do that. It happened because I spent extra time studying and doing my homework.

In the meantime, some of my peers made fun of me for not attending recreational activities as they thought I should. But it didn't matter to me. I felt better staying home, studying, and getting good grades. That was my focus.

During my high school years, I also received a couple of awards for putting in practice time and improving in band. Playing the tuba was difficult because my teacher could tell if I hadn't practiced every night just by listening to my sound. Not only did I have to practice the tuba in the bathroom at school, but I also had to take it home with me to practice every night.

Transporting the tuba was quite a challenge, but the band teacher had a maintenance shop build a special cart with casters. He strapped the tuba case onto the cart with a bungee cord, making it easier for me to roll it down the hall.

I was also given special permission to use the elevator to move between floors and to go through the dining room kitchen to take my tuba outside. Staff members would guide me through the kitchen, and from there, I could roll my tuba down the sidewalk to the dorms. I had to do this every day during the school year. The only thing I needed was my debit card, but it made it possible for me to practice every night, which I did.

Early morning band practice was sometimes a drag because I had to hurry around to get started, but I managed. I also joined the brass choir, where we practiced various songs. Because of all the time I put into playing the tuba, I received awards twice for my dedication. Then, when I graduated high school, I was honored as the salutatorian, second in my class.

Being named salutatorian was an achievement I could carry with me for the rest of my life, and I still feel proud of it today.

Chapter 7: Beyond the Vision

My blindness has never hindered me from gaining all the skills I needed in life, but it did make it difficult for me to maintain friendships and relationships. I struggled to meet people, form lasting connections, and participate in the social world that seemed to come so easily to everyone else.

I also had problems with friendships and relationships because I struggled to get out there and meet people. I met some individuals in my classes, but I only talked to some of them once or twice.

I might talk to some of them a lot and get to know people that way. But regarding everyone else and their lives, I just couldn't be a part of it. Everyone wanted to go off and do their own thing.

I just didn't think I could be involved in it. I always felt left out. That's how for the most part, relationships were for me while I was in school. I met many classmates with whom I spoke only once or twice, while others I got to know better. But beyond that, I always felt left out. Everyone had their own lives and activities. No matter how much I wanted to, I often found myself on the outside looking in.

I had to fit in everywhere I went. Even the places designed for people like me were the same. The programs designed for blind students weren't much help either. I started a public school program in Oklahoma City, which was supposed to integrate blind students into regular education. Instead, they separated us by placing those who were severely visually impaired or completely blind into a distinct classroom with a specialized teacher.

A Vision of Strength:
The Michael Chronicles

That worked out well in the beginning because I had a teacher who understood what she was doing. But after she retired, the teachers that followed didn't have the same knowledge or training.

By the time I was in fifth grade, my education had already suffered. My parents saw that the program wasn't working and decided that the public school wasn't the right place for me and the other blind students in the program. They were correct because public school was not made for us.

In 1975, I was sent to the *Oklahoma School for the Blind* in Muskogee, a town made famous by *Merle Haggard's* song *"Okie from Muskogee."* Unfortunately, that song had some truth because I spent eight years there, and those eight years were not particularly enjoyable.

I made a few good friends, some of whom I still keep in touch with today, but most of my classmates were not real friends. That's the hardest truth to digest.

Many of them made fun of me. The biggest dilemma, however, was that most of the school's students had some degree of vision. Only two or three of us were utterly blind, and the staff didn't understand how to teach students who had never had sight.

A Vision of Strength:
The Michael Chronicles

In hindsight, there were many problems. They could be easily fixed, but no one bothered, as they didn't want to step out of their comfort zones.

Basic things would get complicated. They couldn't explain colors to someone who had never seen them, and they struggled to teach orientation and mobility because they didn't know how to describe a street layout to someone without a frame of reference.

When I asked questions, they often didn't have answers. I struggled with abstract reasoning, shapes, and even reading Braille correctly. My letters and numbers were usually reversed, but no one figured out why. And I wasn't the only one the school failed. Almost everyone had struggles that went unaddressed.

For example, there was a student who had hearing impairments and cognitive challenges in addition to being blind. One day, I sat next to him at the table trying to have breakfast, and he said to a staff member, *"I see double."* And that staff member said, *"Oh, good. Are you including Florida? Oh, good, Kendall."* I still couldn't understand why that happened.

A Vision of Strength:
The Michael Chronicles

It might have been funny if one of us had said it as a joke, but this was a staff member who should have known better. He needed help, and she ignored him. That was just plain sad.

Another student, *Will*, used only one hand. Yet, the only guidance he ever got was, *"Use your good hand, Will."* That was all he ever heard from the staff. No one took the time to teach him how to adapt to his disability.

Then there was *Yogi*, whose real name was *Yogish*. His family, originally from India, didn't know what to do with a blind child, so they did nothing. When he arrived at the school, the staff assumed he was mentally retarded and dismissed him entirely. He eventually left early because they gave up on him. When I talked to him years later, his only words about the experience were, *"I hated it."*

There's more to this, but these little stories are meant to help one understand that the school not only did things wrong with me back in the 80s when I was there but also got it wrong with pretty much everyone. It was incredibly sad.

I graduated as a salutatorian, achieving good grades and feeling proud that I had come in almost first and outperformed everyone. Even though they might have won the award if they had put in more effort, it's possible they could have achieved it on their own.

The rehab center in *Little Rock, Arkansas*, was the next place I got in, but it didn't work out for me. While I was there, it was known as *Arkansas Enterprises for the Blind*. The issue was that these people in Arkansas were accustomed to taking in people once they lost sight. The moment I came to them, they never understood how to work with someone who never had their sight. It manifested itself well; *I tried to learn how to walk around. I did everything on my own there.*

They call it orientation and mobility. What it meant was that I couldn't quite understand how the streets, blocks, and everything were supposed to be laid out. It came down to the other system that we were all supposed to read, *Braille*. I'm good at it. I can even get a book from the library and sit down to read it.

But I could never write with the tool they wanted, a *stylus*. You held this little stylus and pressed it into this tiny device with grooves called a *slate*. I always had to work extra hard to form the letters correctly, but as they say, practice makes perfect. It remained the toughest thing for me despite all the practice.

I had to mentally focus on forming each letter. By the end of the night, I felt mentally exhausted after working with it. It was like someone asking you to speak, but you struggled to find the words, and it never got any easier. You could say it was like trying to explain to someone who could never hear how words are meant to be spoken, yet being told to talk anyway, and they couldn't do it.

But I could never truly settle in during that time. Many people would tell me I was goofing around and that I didn't belong in college, but I chose to ignore those voices and went anyway. However, this program in Arkansas never really panned out.

Even though I got through the college prep program because they allowed us to use a tape recorder while taking the English class, they said most professors would enable us to record the classes.

I used to take the recorder. I listened to the recordings afterward and even got with other students in the class. I tried to study with them a little and did the work of writing the papers, using a typewriter, and handing them in. Despite all the tries, I earned a C in the class, which allowed me to pass, and those credits transferred to *East Central University* in *Ada*, where I attended college.

The rehab staff suggested I stay longer, but one intern was honest with me and said, *"Mike, you should probably just go on to college. Staying here won't help you much."* He was right. I stayed a little longer, but it didn't make much difference.

It was about December 1983 when I left *Arkansas Enterprises* for the Blind and started college. I later returned in 1990, when the program had changed its name to Lions World, supported by the Lions Club.

I went through their evaluation again and tried to train for a taxpayer service representative job, but I didn't qualify because I couldn't read Braille fast enough.

I was told I could try again, but after working to improve my skills, I realized I wouldn't reach the required level. My rehab counselor was supportive, but she also warned me that if I stayed too long out of school and failed to get a job, I wouldn't be able to return to college.

Faced with that clear-cut reality, I chose to go back to school and finish my degree instead.

A Vision of Strength:
The Michael Chronicles

Lions World eventually rebranded as World Services for the Blind, but the programs remained largely the same. They are still focused on helping people adjust to blindness after losing sight. Experts might argue that their methods work for those who were blind from birth, but my experience says otherwise. I went through their programs, and they never really worked for me.

I kept pushing forward. I finished school, even though I knew there might not be anything for me at the end. At least in college, I had a familiar environment where I learned how to function. That was the important thing. But the loneliness never entirely went away. My disability didn't just make academics harder; it made essential human relationships difficult. And that was something no program ever truly prepared me for.

Being blind from birth has changed my life in many ways. Still, one of the most challenging aspects has always been relationships, not just romantic relationships, but friendships, casual acquaintances, and even small simple day-to-day interactions with strangers.

The world is built on visual cues, unspoken signals, body language, and eye contact. Without those, I feel like I've spent my entire life trying to navigate conversations and social situations in the dark while everyone else has a map.

People often assume that blindness only affects mobility and independence, but what they don't realize is that it also isolates you in a much deeper way. It creates a barrier between you and the rest of the world, not just in the physical sense, but in how people engage with you, how they view you, and how they decide to include or exclude you.

I always felt like I was standing just outside the circle, listening to the laughter, conversations, and connections being made but never fully being a part of it.

One of the biggest struggles I've faced is the way people communicate with me. Because I don't have eye contact or can pick up on subtle facial expressions, I rely entirely on the tone of voice, words, and the way someone speaks. We all have a way of living our lives. They nod instead of saying *"yes."* They shrug instead of saying, *"I don't know."* They smile to reassure you. They frown to show sympathy. They wave or gesture instead of calling your name. And when they realize I can't see those things, they don't always adjust how they communicate they just stop trying. There were many things I could never witness.

A Vision of Strength:
The Michael Chronicles

There have been countless times when I've been part of a conversation but not really included in it. People will speak around me, not to me. They'll forget I'm there because I'm not making eye contact. They'll assume I'm uninterested because I'm not reacting like a sighted person would.

Even when I try to engage, to insert myself into the conversation, I can feel hesitation, the awkwardness, the uncertainty in their voices. They don't know how to talk to me, so *they just... don't.*

Friendships were complicated growing up. In school, everyone had their groups, their routines, their unspoken understanding of how to interact. They'd make eye contact across the room, signaling plans for after class. They'd pass notes with just a glance. They'd pick up on social dynamics and body language that I was completely unaware of. And because I couldn't be a part of those silent conversations, I was left out of the spoken ones, too.

It wasn't that people were cruel, at least not always. It was just that they didn't know how to include me. They weren't sure what I could do, where I fit in, and how to make me part of the group without feeling forced. So, instead of making the effort, they carried on without me.

A Vision of Strength:
The Michael Chronicles

Even the friends I made had their limits. They were kind, talked to me, and spent time with me, but only to a point. I was left behind when it came time to do things that required sight, going to the movies, playing sports, and passing notes in class. I was always deprived of such normal day stuff. They didn't do it to be mean, but they didn't stop thinking about how it felt for me.

Romantic relationships were even harder. Most people connect through a combination of attraction, shared experiences, and social cues. But for me, attraction wasn't based on looks. It was based on personality, how someone spoke, and how they treated me. That made it difficult because, in a world that places so much value on appearances, I could not know what people saw in me or what they didn't.

People often assumed I couldn't date at all, as if blindness somehow made me incapable of love. Others saw me as someone to pity, not someone to be in a relationship with. And even when I did find someone interested in me, there was always the underlying question: was it because they actually liked me, or because they felt sorry for me? Were they with me because they wanted to be, or because they thought they were doing a good deed?

A Vision of Strength:
The Michael Chronicles

There's also the issue of how people treat you when you have a disability. Some go out of their way to be overly helpful, assuming you can't do anything alone. Others avoid you altogether, afraid of saying or doing the wrong thing. And then some treat you like you don't exist at all. They talk to the person you're with instead of talking to you. They assume you have nothing to contribute, nothing to say, nothing worth listening to.

I can't count how many times I've visited a restaurant. It's truly exhausting, constantly proving that you're more than your disability. That you have thoughts, opinions, feelings, and dreams. That you can contribute to a conversation, that you can hold your own, that you can be just as much a part of the world as anyone else. But no matter how hard you try, there will always be those who see you as different. As someone less. As someone to be pitied rather than understood.

Over the years, I've learned to navigate these challenges. I've found ways to communicate more effectively, to make people see me for who I am rather than what I lack. I've built friendships with those who truly understand and accept me. But the loneliness never fully goes away. There will always be moments when I feel like I'm on the outside looking in, like the world is happening around me rather than with me.

Blindness isn't just about not seeing. It's about how the world treats you because you can't see. It involves continuously explaining, adapting, and advocating for inclusion in a society that still doesn't completely grasp what it means to be blind.

But despite everything, I continue to try. I keep reaching out, forming connections, and demonstrating that I have as much to offer as anyone else. Because at the end of the day, that's all we want: to be seen, heard, and included. I did my best to make things easier for myself.

Chapter 8: Out of Sight, Overlooked

It was in undergraduate school when I realized that my history degree would not provide promising job prospects. During that time, *I started looking at things in a different light.* The challenge was twofold: *first, being aware of available job interviews, and second, being able to access them independently.*

I had a lot on my hands, knowing I hadn't many opportunities available. I prepared a resume while still in school and sent it to 13 different offices.

That was just the beginning.

A Vision of Strength:
The Michael Chronicles

I struggled to find and apply for jobs. Even if I could identify opportunities, I questioned my ability to perform those roles. My rehabilitation counselor, who was supposed to assist me, did not provide any help, leaving me to go through this process all alone.

Throughout college, I constantly worried about my career prospects. Whenever I asked others about job opportunities with a history major and a sociology minor, they all told me that, inevitably, teaching was the only option.

The thought of teaching would stress me out to no end. Standing in a classroom full of students with no clue where to begin, I had difficulty maintaining discipline. My advisor suggested avoiding the teaching track but guided me through the coursework required for a history degree.

My family was supportive throughout that whole period. I first consulted my mother and stepdad about everything. They advised me to complete my degree without worrying too much about employment.

I enjoyed my studies and felt accomplished upon graduation, although I sometimes questioned the value of my efforts. Nevertheless, I took pride in the experience and education I gained.

A Vision of Strength:
The Michael Chronicles

Upon completing my master's degree, I planned to pursue vocational rehab counseling and find a job. However, as I approached the end of my program, my rehab counselor cautioned that even with the degree, job opportunities would be limited. She recommended trying out a taxpayer service representative program at a rehab center or returning to school if that didn't work out.

After some thought, I decided to try the taxpayer service representative program. Unfortunately, I didn't enjoy the role and realized I didn't want to return to school either. A staff member at the Arkansas rehab center suggested I either drop out and return for further training or force myself to stay in school. I chose to return to the rehab center to improve my skills.

I requested and completed a vocational evaluation, which yielded no positive outcomes. Thankfully, a supportive counselor at the rehab center intervened, advocating for a different evaluation method. They assessed me by placing me on the main switchboard to observe my learning and adaptability. I also requested a vocational evaluation and took it. The vocational review didn't come up with anything positive for me.

A Vision of Strength:
The Michael Chronicles

Luckily, this counselor I had at the rehab center stood up for me. He got on the phone, talked to my counselor, and said, *"We knew that this test we just gave Mike was outdated."*

He said, "My suggestion is that *you let Mike stay here as long as you plan for him too and let us evaluate him differently."*

After he spoke to my state council about it, she agreed to let me stay down there and be evaluated differently. They assessed me by placing me on the main switchboard to see how I learned and if I could operate it. It turned out that I could operate it, learn it, and do it even though I had some challenges.

Well, that was one of those things I started doing all along. But, anyway, I wanted to return to school with their own shop. I got back to school and got back into graduate school. Once I got back to school, I knew I had to finish.

Regardless of the initial challenges, I accomplished everything and received a positive recommendation to retry the taxpayer service representative role. However, I decided instead to return to school.

A Vision of Strength:
The Michael Chronicles

Once back home, after the holidays, I informed my counselor of my decision to re-enroll. She cautioned me about the limited job prospects post-graduation but approved my return. Determined, I re-entered graduate school and committed to completing my degree despite moments of doubt.

During my graduate studies, my counselor advised me to finish each semester if I ever considered dropping out again. I continued through the spring semester, attended summer school, and persisted through the fall, fulfilling all coursework requirements.

My counselor once told me, *"Mike, if you're going to drop out of school again, you probably want to finish the semester first and then go."*

After considering it for a day or two, I decided I had to stick with it, and that's precisely what I did. I completed the spring semester, attended summer school, and continued this throughout the semester.

With that, I had a clear path in mind. I completed my classwork for my degree. The only other requirement was an internship. After a few attempts in Oklahoma, I went to Dallas, Texas, where I finished the internship right there.

Chapter 9: Brittle Bonds

I could say I had it a bit easier growing up with a disability than most people. While I got all the support from my family, the world, on the other hand, could be cruel at times.

Growing up with blindness was not comfortable; I always had to keep it together. Out of many people in my life, my stepdad was always there, guiding me through every encounter with patience, kindness, and unwavering support.

A Vision of Strength:
The Michael Chronicles

When he entered my life, he said he would stand by me no matter what. He wasn't just a parental figure; *he became my mentor, advocate, and biggest source of encouragement.*

In my mind, my stepdad never hesitated to step up. Even when I graduated high school, he was there to assure me I could still have memorable experiences, even with my visual impairment.

He took my mom and me on a road trip in a camper van to Oregon, where we visited family and explored places I wouldn't have otherwise had the chance to see.

Even when I had to leave that trip early to fly back for a college prep program, he made everything smooth and made sure that I had everything I needed to achieve. His support just didn't stop there. As I continued through college, he was always thinking ahead, helping me set up my living spaces, making sure I had the right technology to complete my work, and even finding me a proper desk to study efficiently.

During the melting summers, when I struggled with math or needed extra credit, he worked on my papers, always just being there and guiding me in many ways. It all came very easily to him.

A Vision of Strength:
The Michael Chronicles

When my mother fell ill, he took on even more responsibilities, balancing his job while caring for her and making sure I was supported both emotionally and practically.

He kept our family together, aiming for a good life so I could focus on my studies while also preparing me for the inevitable hardships ahead. Times weren't easy for him when my mom got sick with each passing day.

Even during the darkest moments, like when my mother's illness worsened, he continued to be my rock, making sure I was never alone in my grief. His capacity to handle everything that came his way and became strong for my mother and me left a lasting impact on my life.

His presence changed my education and independence and how I viewed devotion and kindness. He made every major transition in my life, from school to internships to eventually navigating life after graduate school, smoother.

He taught me that blindness was not a limitation but a challenge to be met with determination. Looking back, I realize how much of my success was built upon his quiet yet steadfast support.

A Vision of Strength:
The Michael Chronicles

My stepdad never received recognition for all that he did. He simply did what needed to be done, ensuring that I was never left behind, never left without guidance, and always knew that someone believed in me. He was more than just a stepfather. He was the person who showed me that, despite my blindness, I could achieve anything with the proper support and determination.

It all dates back to when I met him in 1978. I remember when I was home from school and attended meetings with my mom. She belonged to a religious group; *I believe it was the wellness center*. That's where they first met. My mom and I went to those meetings. I think it was during the summer that we met *Charles Simon*, who would become my stepdad. We just participated in the meetings and did the activities first.

Right after that, he started coming over for meals. I got closer to him, and we got to know each other. Then, it was time for me to return to school, and while I was there, my mom and stepdad became closer. There were some weekends when I could come home.

Fortunately, he moved in during the middle of summer on a particularly hot day. I helped him with the move; *it was both an adventure and a bit of work, but I got it done, and he expressed his gratitude for my assistance.* That's when we began to get to know each other better.

Starting in the summer, when he was off work, and my mom had to go to work, we would have lunch together. Sometimes, he would take me out for lunch, which was a great experience and a lot of fun.

Things got better for me when my stepdad moved in, I was preparing to start my first year of high school. However, my bedroom was too hot to sleep in when I came home, so my stepdad set up a tent in the backyard.

I would go out to the tent every night, lay down, and sleep. We had a little hammock in the tent, and my sleeping bag was fun. It was nice and cool at night when I went out to lie down and go to bed or sleep.

When morning arrived, it was delightful to hear the sounds of nature. I entered the house, had coffee, practiced, and completed our daily activities. Towards the end of summer, my mom and dad discussed things and decided we had to install air conditioning at home because it was becoming almost too hot for us to handle.

A Vision of Strength:
The Michael Chronicles

I struggled to deal with it. I often felt like lying down and going to sleep. It wasn't delightful, especially since the house was always so hot. So, towards the end of summer, we got air conditioning, which made a difference, although we still weren't getting quite enough airflow upstairs to cool things down.

We had the guy come out and install the air conditioning and look at things, and he recommended having an extra extension from the ducts where the plates are working out. They put in the air vents, going around the side of the house and upstairs. The fan would push air up at that extension upstairs, and we could get some cool air in my room at the time; it didn't have any vents.

The next couple of summers that I got to come home from school, I ended up working some summer jobs. During those times that I had those summer jobs, my stepdad would take me to work and come and get me and bring me back home.

It was a good experience. Then, it came time for me to graduate from high school. My stepdad, mom, and I went on vacation after high school. We got in this camper van and went out to Oregon. We visited with my stepdad's mom, who lived in Eugene. Then we drove on into Portland, and it was my stepdad's brother. For me, it was truly a memorable trip.

I had to get on an airplane and fly back to Oklahoma because I was supposed to attend a college prep program in Arkansas. I wasn't looking forward to that, but I knew I had to do it. My younger sister, her boyfriend, and I were out on the airplane and flew back to Oklahoma.

Then, my biological dad met us at the airport and took my sister and her boyfriend back to their place. After that, we stopped by my mom's house to pick up the things I had packed for the college prep program. Once I finished the college prep program, my mom and my stepdad came to get me and brought me back home.

As it happened, I found that the bed and I grew a bit closer during the time between returning home from college prep and the challenging decision to go back to the rehab center for an extended stay. After completing my first semester in college, it was finally time for me to return home.

My mom and sister came to get me, and I spent my first summer home from college with my mom. I wished to have more time with my biological dad that summer. He was home for at least part of the summer when I was there, and we managed to spend some time together.

We did a few things together. We went out for lunch a couple of times, and then I mentioned that they had prepared some meals for us at home. After that, he sent me shopping for a few things I needed, including replacement batteries for my talking watch and similar items.

Finally, it was time for me to return to school, and we experienced some confusion at first about the right day to be back. We also had to discuss with the staff when the college dorm would be open, but eventually, we sorted it out. If I had arrived a day later due to the intense storm, we would have already been open, and I would have been able to unload my things and settle into my room.

But we got it, we got it all worked out. They took me back to what I had done the very next day. I got settled in. I got through my spring and not spring but fall and spring semesters. And we had another summer or two at home where we spent time together.

That same year, I had to go back to summer school because there was a math class I couldn't pass. I had to be away from my mom and stepdad for most of the summer, but it was something I needed to do. My summer school session lasted from June to part of July, and it turned out I would have to come home after I passed my math course.

But that was some time. Then I said I spent time together as I got home, and then we had to figure out what we would do with my stuff because, I found out, the dorm I stayed in during the summer didn't pass fire inspection.

But everything turned out well because the application I had submitted to get into single-student housing had come through, and I could move right into the room I'd be staying in for the rest of my time in college. It turned out to be a good place because I had my own room and even my bathroom. That was what I needed while I was in school, especially during my junior and senior years.

I needed to study and write papers, and my mom and stepdad had got me a computer desk. I went down there, and I think I was trying. I believe my mom was able to come with us. But once we got there, I had to ask a college friend to help us move things up to my room, which we did. I stayed there and assembled the desk, which worked nicely for my computer, printer, and other items.

A Vision of Strength:
The Michael Chronicles

I got through my junior and senior years in college, graduated, and came home to be with my mom and stepdad for a while, but I had to attend summer school. Unfortunately, during my senior year, when I graduated, my mom was diagnosed with breast cancer.

When that happened, my stepdad brought me back to school for my first graduate school summer. While we were going down to where I was going to school, he told me that if my mom got to the point where she couldn't help me with any of the money that she's helped me with, she's helped extend me for going to school, and he would be working with me on that. It was, and it turned out to be okay.

My mom got through her long list of treatments, kept working, and helped me get the money that I needed for school. And it worked out in my favor. After that first summer of graduate school, I started and got through the first two semesters. Then, I had to go home for a little bit of the summer with my mom and my stepdad, but it turned out that I was in graduate school during the summer.

Instead, they had to work during the summers because there were some projects or things they were doing at the place where he worked that he needed to work on. Things had a pattern by then. He would have to go to work that summer, and I'd have to be home alone.

I was able to work out putting lunch together and had talking books to listen to and things like that. And then I wasn't home that long, and it was time for me to go to the rehab center because I had elected to go down there and try and get my skills up and try out for.

During that time, he had some time off from work, and he was able to spend some time at home with me. He told me it was probably a good idea to get back to school and ensure I stayed with it. The economy wasn't doing very well then, so I was better off returning to school, which I did.

My stepdad helped me get my things together and organize them for going back to school. And then, when it was time for me to return to school, they took me. My mom and my dad both took me back to school, and it was. That's how I got through that semester, and it turned out that when it was, I had to go to summer school. I was still able to spend some time together during that summer.

Both at the beginning of the summer before I started the summer school program and in 1991. We got through that summer school.

A Vision of Strength:
The Michael Chronicles

In all honesty, it was engaging and fun, too, getting to visit with some of my friends. But when I got home, my stepdad helped me work on a paper on which I needed the extra credit to help me get the full graduate stipend for school. But when I got home, he still needed to work during the summer, so he took that paper to work with him.

If the paper had ended up on his computer system, he could bring the file I had with him because we were both using *WordPerfect* at the time.

He could work with the paper and make it look better. He printed it out, showed it, and told me about it. Then we put it in an envelope and returned it to Aiden, my teacher. He basically told me afterward that I did well and that my paper for extra credit went through. I got a B on it, and it all worked out. But before we knew it, it was over, and it was time for me to return to school.

I hated going back, but this will be my last semester in Ada at school. I returned and completed the semester, and it turned out that it was time for me to move entirely out of the room I had been in for school. That was not easy, but it turned out my stepdad was the one who took me down there and helped me move out. It took us a whole day to do it. We went down with the van that my folks had, and we loaded everything up into it.

Then we worked on my dorm room and got it back to the point where it kind of looked like it did before I moved in. We cleaned it up as best as we could, and then we brought all my stuff back home. A couple of weeks later, we had to load the van back up and move me down to McAllister, where I was supposed to do an internship.

After the internship didn't work out, I had to come back home and stay home for a while. Then, I said they had helped me move to Dallas, where I had to finish my internship with the Texas Commission for the Blind. I successfully finished that up, finished up the internship, and came home, and it was when I came home.

I finished school. I stayed there and talked about it some more, and he called the people at VOTEC. Then, I think he called the lady who was a teacher at the VOTEC campus in Oklahoma City and decided for us to visit. He went ahead and visited, and the teacher got to know me and discussed everything with me. We arranged for me to go ahead and enroll.

A Vision of Strength:
The Michael Chronicles

I began computer training at VOTEC. When I started, I had to wake up really early, wash up, eat breakfast, walk to the end of our driveway, and catch the school bus that took me to the Vocat campus.

I had to get up real early Monday through Friday, I would catch the bus. I went to VOTEC and got home a little after 3:00 in the afternoon. I did this Monday through Friday, and then my stepdad would come home from work between 4:30 and 5:00. He would check in with my mom to see if she was ready to come home. After that, he would pick her up and bring her home so she could rest before our evening meal. Then, I had to go to bed early so I could wake up and do it all over again. But in '93, I believe, my mom received some bad news at a doctor's visit.

It turned out that her cancer returned in her liver and lungs, and she was able to work a bit through the summer. However, she became very ill and ended up in the hospital. I started VOTEC again around September, but it was a little different this time. I had to get up, get myself ready, go to school, and come back home. My mom came to the hospital, and she wasn't able to work; she was in bed.

A Vision of Strength:
The Michael Chronicles

Then I had to leave when I got home. I needed to check with my mom to see if she needed anything, like ice water or other supplies. I had to check on her. Because of all the medication my mom was on, it became my responsibility to answer the phone when I got home and speak to anyone, including doctors and others. I usually arrived home between 4:30 and 5:00. After I got home, he would take over and figure out what needed to be done.

Evenings grew long and lonely because I had to eat dinner by myself while my stepdad was with my mom. It felt overwhelmingly sad and isolating as my mom was deteriorating. I wasn't going to like it. Over time, my mom began to dislike it too, and it only got worse. November 1993 was approaching, and it would be Armistice Day.

I stepped in and said, *"Well, since you're going to be staying home, I have to. I still have to go to work. We need to be alert to the people in your mom's office. They're going to come by and bring her lunch."* It was a fun day on Veterans Day because I got to stay home.

I knew when the people from my mom's office would arrive, so I went downstairs to wait for them at the door and let them in. They brought a watch for my mom, and we all sat in our bedroom to chat. It was enjoyable. Mom, the lady from the office, and I shared lunch, and it was a great time.

I sat there and came home, then he took over from there and completed our evening routine. The next day was my time to return to school, but Veterans Day would be the last day I could enjoy a good visit with my mom. I wanted to spend time with her before she declined very quickly. It turned out my mom had already asked my stepdad to look for me when she was gone.

I stood there, and he had already talked to me about it. In fact, on a Sunday evening, we went out to dinner, and he told me during the middle of my meal about what was going on and what he was going to do.

But it turned out that from that time on, since we had Veterans Day, she started to get worse and worse. Then, one afternoon, when I came home from school, my stepdad was there, along with the people from the hospice service.

They spoke with my mom, assessed her needs, and arranged everything. Then, the hospice staff would come in to care for her so my stepdad and I could go out and do a few things, like have lunch on Saturday and take care of any shopping we needed.

A Vision of Strength:
The Michael Chronicles

By then, Thanksgiving arrived, and it was a very difficult time because my mom had reached the point of passing away. I was going to school and coming home, but my mom could no longer communicate with us. My stepdad was working as a psychologist for the Yukon School Board. We had to keep an eye on my mom and ensure she took her medications and all that. However, it was becoming increasingly sad and challenging.

We had our Thanksgiving dinner from a dinner that people in my mom's office had sent us. It was myself, my youngest sister, and my stepdad who enjoyed our Thanksgiving dinner, and we gave my mom what Thanksgiving dinner she was able to handle at the time. But she had gotten to the point where she was going in and out of consciousness and passing away.

The day after Thanksgiving was tough for everyone. I was sitting with my mom. I instantly knew things were wrong as her breathing felt different.

In the hospice, people came to check on my mom and see how she was doing. It turned out that we got through the day after Thanksgiving, but on that evening, my mom passed away. She was *gone*. My dad, sister, and I had some leftover

A Vision of Strength:
The Michael Chronicles

Thanksgiving dinner Friday evening. I still thought I needed to check on Mom and see what was happening with her.

He went upstairs to check on her, then came back and told us she was gone. I went upstairs, and my sister asked me if he had ever touched a dead person before. I said I hadn't felt weird when I finally touched my mom. It was strange, and I freaked out a little. But then, after getting through that Friday night, I got up and went downstairs, where my stepdad told me he cared about me.

He wanted me to stay in the house with him, feeling we could get through losing my mom together. So, we got things started; he moved some furniture around, and we began to move on with our lives. Then, the following Monday came, and it was time for me to return to school, which I did. However, I wasn't ready to focus on the schoolwork I needed to tackle, at least not that Monday, just after my mom passed away. The teacher told me that day, *"Mike, you didn't have to come to school."*

But I did. It turned out that on the second day after I returned to school, we started working on the things I needed to focus on. My teacher began helping me, and then that Friday, during the first week back, we had the memorial service for my mom where she worked. I was glad that my teacher from the school biotech program attended the service.

The service was hard, but it was a good one. It was that Friday. Then they had another memorial service that following Sunday at the place where she had gone, close to going to church. She had a service there at a place called the *Water Center* when they buried part of our ashes there.

The following week, my stepdad got off work early, and I came home from school. We got in the car, took part of my mom's ashes, and went to a place she liked in Oklahoma called Red Rock Canyon to bury her ashes together. He took me to the spot where we would scatter the ashes, and he had me hold the bag to dump some out while he did part of it too. It was an interesting trip; i*t was a fun trip*. That's how it was for us since the very first day.

When it came to job opportunities, my stepdad said, "If you can somehow get a job, you can, but if you can't, then you don't have to."

My stepdad and I discussed the computer training, which was based on an operating system that was already outdated.

A Vision of Strength:
The Michael Chronicles

Times were changing. They were transitioning to Windows, but there was no screen-reading software available. At that time, there weren't any job opportunities for me. So, I switched to VOTEC in June but still haven't found any employment opportunities in that area.

I ended up finishing with VOTEC. And then I shipped it, and I went into this period where he still had to go to work, and I had to be home by myself Monday through Friday. I always knew how to keep myself occupied.

My stepdad kept working. He went to work throughout the school years of 1994 and 1995. Then, in the spring, he retired.

He had to retire because the doctor advised him to do so. The doctor said, *"You can keep working and risk having a stroke, or you can choose to retire."*

After his retirement, we spent much time together at home, which was enjoyable. We had fun. He would take me shopping, and we would pick up our groceries. Then, after getting our groceries, we would go home and put them away.

We used to go out for lunch every Monday through Friday, and on weekends, we'd have one meal out on Saturday and another on Sunday. But after the year 2000, money started getting tight. We had to cut back, only going out on weekends. It turned out that the investments my stepdad had arranged for my mom had either run out or failed us.

I never knew all the details because he wasn't the kind to explain everything. I just knew that things had gone bad, and we no longer had the financial freedom we once had. But we adjusted. We did our grocery shopping together, and he'd take me on errands to the bank and post office. Life settled into a steady rhythm until 2006, when everything changed.

That year, my stepdad was diagnosed with prostate cancer. My younger sister moved back home to help him through treatments, and in time, he recovered. But the relief was short-lived. Medical bills began piling up, and the insurance didn't cover everything. Money was tight again.

This time, he maxed out my credit cards and stopped paying. More health problems followed, and while doctors were able to manage them, the financial strain only deepened. The house began falling into disrepair.

February came, and our central air conditioning unit failed. He never fixed it, but we managed with two large window units. We devised a system turning them on late in the morning, shutting them off during peak hours due to an energy program, and then switching them back on in the evening. We made it work, we always did.

By 2018, more health issues surfaced. He underwent cataract surgery and struggled with worsening sinus problems. Despite all that, we still found ways to keep our routine. We planned our meals together, shopped for groceries, and I helped him with daily tasks. Eventually, the doctors scheduled him for sinus surgery to help with his breathing issues. But before that could happen, those very issues overtook him.

That Father's Day came and went. Days later, on June 19, I went to check on him. He didn't respond. Something felt wrong. When I looked closer, I realized he wasn't breathing. No air came from his mouth, no rise or fall in his chest. I tried mouth-to-mouth resuscitation and CPR, but deep down, I knew. The gurgling sound I had heard from him in the days prior suddenly made sense that he had suffocated in his sleep, likely from the sinus drainage.

I called 911 right away. The paramedics arrived, followed by the police. They asked their questions, but it was clear that this was just the natural course of life taking someone too soon. No foul play. Nothing suspicious. Just loss. The funeral home was called, and they took him away. It was final.

At the funeral, the staff handed me their cards before they left. I called someone who had been helping me with various things. He came over and looked at my stepdad's belongings. Then, I called my youngest sister. She came to get me. We took the dogs to a boarding kennel, had a meal together, and then I left with her. I stayed at her house that night, heavy with the weight of it all.

Losing my stepdad wasn't just losing a person. It was losing the structure of my daily life, the one person who had been beside me in all the little, ordinary moments. In the silence he left behind, I realized how much of my world had been built around him. In the days that followed, I learned that grief isn't just an overwhelming wave all on.

It's in the small spaces, too. Every quiet meal and errand once shared, without his voice calling me along. Somehow, life had to go on. And somehow, I had to find a way to keep moving forward.

A Vision of Strength:
The Michael Chronicles

At the funeral, the people at the funeral home gave me their cards. After they left, I called the guy who was helping me with some different things.

He came to the house and looked at my stepdad's things. Then I called my youngest sister, and she came and got me. We left with the dogs that my stepdad had, put them in a boarding kennel, and went out for a meal. And then, I ended up staying at my youngest sister's house. After my mother's loss, that day was the heaviest one for me.

Chapter 10: Ability to Live with a Disability

Life doesn't always unfold how we expect it to. We find ways to adapt, push forward, and make the most of what we have.

Being blind in 1963 meant growing up in a world that wasn't designed for people like me. There were no talking devices, apps to read labels, or the Internet to look up information.

The resources that exist today *simply* weren't available, and that meant learning through trial and error, often relying on others more than I wanted to.

From a young age, I understood that if I was going to live independently, I had to figure things out for myself in a world that didn't always think about people like me.

As a child, I didn't fully understand what being blind meant. No one sat me down and explained it to me. I was eight years old before I even realized I was completely blind, and by then, I had already begun to pull back from things other kids took for granted.

My mother discovered my blindness within my first year, and much later, I learned that it was caused by medication she had taken during pregnancy. But in those early years, none of that mattered. What mattered was that I was a kid trying to make sense of the world without sight, and the tools to help me do that were few and far between.

Public school was a challenge. I was placed in a class with other blind and partially sighted students, but there were no specialized tools to help us learn.

A Vision of Strength:
The Michael Chronicles

My first teacher did her best, and I managed to get by, though I struggled with Braille and reversing letters. But things worsened in fourth and fifth grade when our teachers didn't know how to teach blind students.

I fell behind, frustrated and discouraged. In sixth grade, we finally got a teacher who understood what we needed, but by then, I had already lost valuable time. Resources for blind students were scarce, and we were left to make do with whatever little support was available.

At age 12, I was sent to a school for the blind. There, I finally caught up on reading, though I remained a slow reader. I learned daily living skills like taking care of my clothes, cooking, and even something as simple as eating properly with a knife and fork.

High school introduced even more independence. Living in a dorm, we cooked our meals, learning through hands-on experience rather than modern instructional videos or accessible guides. Twice a week, we made dinner; five days a week, we cooked breakfast. It wasn't always easy, but it was the first real taste of self-sufficiency.

A Vision of Strength:
The Michael Chronicles

After high school, I attended a rehab center in Arkansas previously known as Lions World, later renamed Arkansas Enterprises for the Blind.

The training there was basic: *preparing meals, cooking, and practicing life skills.* Times were tough then; *for someone with a disability, there was little to no accessibility.* There were no accessible apps, no screen readers—just repetition and patience. A rehab teacher helped me navigate the campus when I went to college.

There were no GPS systems or digital maps, so I memorized routes and relied on landmarks. The cafeteria became my main source of meals, as cooking independently wasn't something I could manage easily without accessible tools.

After college, I moved back home with my stepdad in Oklahoma City. During the day, while he worked, I prepared microwave meals. When he retired, he took over meal preparation but always ensured I was involved. We shopped together, picking out groceries as best we could without any apps to read labels.

I relied on his descriptions, touch, and memory. We experimented with slow cooker meals, then moved to stove and oven cooking, though it wasn't long before we went back to the slow cooker for safety reasons.

When I later moved in with my dad for two years, I faced another set of challenges. He was strict about keeping me away from the stove, convinced it was too dangerous. I had received a little training in using a stove back in Oklahoma City through a rehab teacher, and I had successfully used my sister's oven with her guidance.

But my dad wouldn't allow it, reinforcing that certain things weren't meant for people like me. There were no accessible cooking tutorials, no easy ways to prove to him that I could handle it. So, I adapted once again, using the microwave and the convection oven he had given me, marking it as best I could.

When COVID hit, I was stuck at my dad's place longer than expected. Eventually, I moved back into my own home, but shortly after, my dad got sick and passed away. Living alone was an adjustment, but by then, technology had started to bridge the gap between what was possible and what had once been impossible for blind individuals.

My sister, who has been a good help to me, moved in with me for almost a year, helping with groceries and cooking.

A Vision of Strength:
The Michael Chronicles

Even after she moved out, she continued to assist with shopping.

We started using the Walmart app to order groceries, a luxury that didn't exist in my younger years. Instead of struggling to read food labels by touch or memory, I could now use *Seeing AI* or *Be My Eyes* to scan and identify items. Sometimes, it made multiple attempts, but it was still a world of difference from the past.

Transportation was another area where things had changed. In the early years, I had to rely entirely on family or friends, scheduling rides far in advance. Now, I pay friends who do transportation on the side, giving me more flexibility. This has made things easier for me to no end.

My sister still helps me get to the bank and post office, as my apartment's outdoor mailboxes aren't secure due to the area's high crime rate. I can do things alone on my own now, from getting around my complex, taking out the trash, visiting my sister, and going to the apartment office, but I avoid high-traffic regions for safety reasons.

Amidst all the restrictions and limited resources, *I've managed to carve out a life that works for me.* The tools available today have made a difference, but I still remember what they were like.

Once again, the life I have been living has been easier but too cruel at times. The people at my rehab center doubted I could live independently because I struggled with Braille, slow reading, and letter reversals. But I adapted. My phone now reads text to me, apps help with accessibility, and devices like Google Home and Alexa assist in ways that were unimaginable decades ago.

Being blind doesn't mean you can't live a full life. I know some blind people who do more than me and some who do less. I consider myself somewhere in the middle.

The important thing is not to let limitations define you. We work with what we have, and when new tools become available, we embrace them. I've learned to rely on technology, seek help, and be independent.

Some people still doubt what's possible, but I've proven that if there is no one else, blindness isn't the end of opportunity. It just means finding another way.

Looking back, I think about how much it has changed. As a kid, there was no voice-activated technology, no accessible apps, and no instant way to read a document or identify a product.

Today, I can do all of that with my phone. But the journey hasn't just been about technology; *It's about my own perception of how I view things*. It's about refusing to let the world tell me what I can and can't do. It's about adapting, moving forward, and showing that life is still meant to be fully lived, even without sight.

About the Author

I'm known by the name Michael Irons, born completely blind in 1963, and my life has been a wild ride. Growing up in a world that was clearly not designed for people like me, I faced unusual challenges, but I never let my blindness define who I am or what I could achieve.

I graduated as a salutatorian from high school, earned a bachelor's degree, and later completed a master's degree.

Along the way, I was fortunate to receive several scholarships, which helped fund my education. I also found joy and success in extracurricular activities in various fields; *these very things got me multiple awards for my dedication and progress.*

My life has been deeply molded by the consistent support of my family, especially my stepdad, who became my rock and guiding light in this life. Living in a society that often overlooks the needs of the blind and relies on outdated systems. I didn't let that take over me. I completed internships and vocational training, though the lack of accessible technology made progress difficult at times.

A Vision of Strength:
The Michael Chronicles

Today, I live a much different life, independently, using modern tools like screen-reading apps and voice-activated devices to navigate a world that is finally starting to accommodate people like me.

My story is for all; *anyone who thinks they can't go far in life can read this as a guideline to how life never ceases for one.* In my case, it's about proving that blindness isn't a barrier to achievement; it's just a contest to be met with courage and curiosity to live life on your terms.

www.ingramcontent.com/pod-product-compliance
Lightning Source LLC
Chambersburg PA
CBHW051325120626
46547CB00015B/2394